PLANTED IN SNOW SOAKED GRASS

Christian Emond

BookLeaf Publishing

India | USA | UK

Presentation by *BookLeaf* Publishing

Web: www.bookleafpub.com

E-mail: info@bookleafpub.com

ISBN: 9789358361599

First edition 2021

DEDICATION

In memory of Pappy, a man larger than life, stronger than graphene, and gone too soon for our hearts to bear. My grandfather, a proud and unconditionally loving parent, and an inspiration to those who knew him. Forever loved and never forgotten.

To Sravya, aka Torty the Tortoise, without whom I may have stopped 'having a good time'. I could spend the next infinity talking to you and still want more time to chat. Yours forever moulting, Lobby the Lobster.

For Anika, my number one poetry supporter, without whom I would not have someone to read the pages of this book. I will continue to write so long as you will continue to read.

To Sarah, my favourite frond and collaborator. Thank you for holding me up no matter how bad my skating is and supporting my dreams no matter how fragile they are.

For the reader who may not have found their voice, their 'people', or themselves, keep searching.

Finally, for those who have not let an icy world harden your heart, rather have embraced compassion and empathy. You are the best of us.

ACKNOWLEDGEMENT

This collection could not have been written if I did not have the support of a few influential people in my life who have supported me either in my writing or in continuing to live life, nor without those who have embraced my occasionally crazy ideas.

I would like to start by thanking Sravya Kakumanu, who I have more words for than I have space. She has not only been my best friend (and sea creature friend) she has supported me at my lowest, been understanding of struggles she admits to not knowing anything about, and helped me to celebrate my successes. I would quite literally not be here today without having her in my life and I am lucky to know such an amazing young woman. She is on the road to becoming an amazing doctor and has immense musical and artistic talent, that I wish she shared with the world more.

Thank you to Anika Zaman, who convinced me to continue writing poetry after I had let go of it. She is compassionate, humble, and an amazing writer in her own right, truly a gem of a human being. Anika is incredibly encouraging and the first person to have read the poems in this collection. She will forever be my sounding board for good and bad poetry and I hope one day she receives love equal to the amount she has put out into the world.

Thank you to Sarah Walker, for never shying away from a chance to let me know I am wrong and always letting me know when I am right. I have worked with countless people and will continue to meet new colleagues, but I will never find a replacement for you. I hope we can always find new projects to develop together so I can continue to pick your brain. If it was not for your enthusiasm, wisdom, and perspective on life I would not be the person I am today.

Thank you to my family

My twin sister Jewel, who is too often overlooked for how kind, caring, and talented a person she is. It is a pleasure and an honour to have you as my built in partner in crime. I await to see the spectacle you will make in the next phase of your life.

My mom and dad, who have separately supported my growth in different and equally substantial ways. Thank you for all that you have sacrificed for the two of us, setting your kids up to understand that life is rarely what you expect, and that the world revolves around the sun and not us.

My grandparents for each being someone to learn from. Regardless of how near or far, or the time I have had or lacked to spend with you, know that you have been an influence on the man I am today and will always be in my heart.

Thanks to Christian Kindrachuk a journalist and good friend, who I first traded poems back and forth with years ago. He allowed me to find myself as a writer without judgement or scorn and I regrettably take far too long to write back to him.

Thank you to all of those who have been a part of my journey through the iGEM years, though you may not be listed by name you know who you are. Regardless of if we have kept in touch or are not on speaking terms anymore, you have been influential to my life.

Lastly, I would be remiss to not show appreciation to Andrew Symes who sent me an advertisement for the #WriteYourHeartOut competition on the last day to register. You sir are appreciated more than you know, continue being the 'friendly and kind' guy you are.

Thank you to Alvira and *BookLeaf* Publishing for giving inexperienced and first time writers like myself the opportunity to express themselves and publish their work in an accessible and generous manner. I wish for immense success to the company.

PREFACE

It is a little 'all over the place' isn't it? Well I suppose that's just how thoughts are. In one moment they may be here and in the next they are over there. In fact, in the same moment, I have found many thoughts in one place and everywhere.

The world in 2021 and its, perhaps more ruthless, predecessor 2020, has had a climate of uncertainty and heartbreak, however along with it has come some pockets of serenity and recollection. In this time, I had already been well on the rocky road to self-discovery and learning not only who I was, but how to retrieve the pieces of myself I had mistakenly given to others. The poems found in this collection, thus can be seen as a reflection on this journey and its associated feelings of loss, love, and curiosity. Through suicidal periods, great success, debilitating anxiety, new adventures, loneliness, and getting lost in thought, I have felt the need to 'write my heart out'.

When deciding on a title for this collection I had played with the idea of focusing on 'thought' and 'wonder', as I have felt most poetic in times when I can truly explore my thoughts, whether that be late at night or having a moment of solace in nature. However, the more I thought about what the poems meant to me and why I wrote each of them, I came to see that they were really all connected by ruminations I have had on the pain of my past, the hope of my future, and how I feel lost between the two in the present.

I, perhaps much like you, love being in love, loving someone, and being loved. However, in relationships you may not be happy, healthy, or even have all three cases of love. "Broken Summer" and "This Year" were written in reflection of the emotionally abusive relationship I had with my first love. The former narratively takes place not long after breaking up and the latter is a realization on having found myself happier after moving on. It can be hard to realize when you are in an emotionally abusive relationship, because you rely on this person for emotional support and raise them on a pedestal, easily forgiving them for the pain they cause you. Blinded for years, though the relationship has ended, the trauma lives on in new relationships and memories.

"Snow Soaked Grass" is my favourite and most personal poem. As I tended to the rough greenery in my backyard, the smells of uncovered autumn death, melting winter, and new spring filled my nose and mind with memories I had long forgotten. One memory after the other I was transported to very different eras of my life and thought on how the snow can hold memories or pain (though not synonymous) and are melted in the spring as we either forget or let go. By extension one could think of the water cycle, simply looking at the movement of water from the clouds, to the ground, into plants, and back up to the sky. Water (being used as a metaphor for memories) not only has multiple forms, whether it be a light shower, a dangerous storm, a snowfall or hail, it provides life to plants and allows them to grow. This poem provides a personal touch to realizing in any given moment you have simultaneously grown away from your past and continue to grow toward your future.

I may never truly know who I am, but I will always find myself content knowing I was.

This collection of poetry was made as part of the #WriteYourHeartOut writing challenge for Canada facilitated by Alvira Publishing – the challenge: write 20 poems in 20 days.

1. PLANTED

They say we only grow when it rains.

Like our beloved leafy counterparts who sit in windowsills and in the garden,

We too must accept the environment we are in.

Though not sessile, we are often rooted in one place.

Those who are fortunate will have a sunny sky above their head and a safe space to grow taller.

They will have mutualistic relationships and even reproduce before winter.

I however have been beset by storms and snow.

Gale force winds sheared my stalk,

While debris pummelled my limbs.

Planted in sick soil and attacked by pests,

My environment has been hostile.

Wilted and worn this season has taken its toll.

Yet with the promise of a new spring next year,

I will grow.

2. BROKEN SUMMER

The one to brave the bitter cold

And emerge from the blizzard bold

Will be the one to guide me through

The mist and rain of misfortune.

For there never was a hero

So beaten and bruised

Than the man that loved you.

The light against a sea of dark,

A contrast so beautiful,

Her words always hit their mark.

Further and further did those arrows dig,

Searching for meaning beyond time,

We're caught up in each moment not realising we are sick.

I remember the month of November.

In those days you gave in to anger

And let love slip slowly away.

In those moments I wanted you to stay.

So I fought for us and for revival,

But I was caught up in survival.

Left again to be suffocated in a haze,

Walls towering above me, lost in a maze,

Eventually, I found the centre and found nothing.

So long was I searching I was left with no future tactic,

I sat there in the silence of anti-climax.

The dark reflected back on me and I could see clearly again.

So full was my destruction,

Only Stockholm could explain past action.

Could it be that it was all my own construction?

Stuck so long in my own machinations,

I left the haze and with it you.

Then there it was,

love,

left at the exit,

As if it was only ever a backup plan.

A fail safe if things didn't pan out.

You wanted a hero, but you got me,

Walking away, feeling for the last time, guilty.

I remember when it began in the summer,

But nowadays the fall has become clearer.

With every day the season moves on,

As I inch towards the beginning of a new dawn.

Perhaps one day we'll meet again

And we'll reminisce on our shared edges,

But for now I bid you adieu for all our hedges,

Remember me in the winter.

3. THIS YEAR

This year I spent my days less anxious,

I worried less about hurting you and you leaving me.

I felt more myself, breathing in air as if it was my first time alone.

I scraped my knees and laughed without concern of your reaction.

I fell more times than I can count and regretted nothing.

This year I felt happy when I was with my dad,

I spent time with loved ones too often left aside.

I could smile without a mask and I did so with so much force it hurt,

It made me cry and it made me lose control.

I loved every second laughing with them.

Never did I check my phone and never did I worry about the time.

I found myself in the moment again.

This year I celebrated and felt proud of my accomplishments.

I embraced my friends with affection I couldn't show before.

I opened up and let people in,

Welcoming them to what I found to be me.

I learned what it meant to have supporters

And to have people unafraid to show they love me.

This year I spent time exploring my interests.

I rambled on about my passions to people that listened intently,

And found those with vision and motivation.

I saw more futures than one and no one limited the scope of what I could imagine.

I started to dream again.

This year our anniversary passed and I found myself...

Happier without you.

4. SKETCHBOOK

The skies have shaded into grey,

Threatening the light we go astray.

In search of something blue,

We found nothing true.

For above us is uniform,

A scene turned to storm.

In this, we struggle to hold on,

To make it to a new day's dawn.

The winds leave us breathless

And the lightning thunders through us.

Our lives flashing in and out of reality,

We question how this could be,

Nature on track and me on a crash course.

Through the night I long to find the source

Of this suffering and misery.

I want to leave behind all the pity

And join my company in optimism.

As I fight through my inner schism,

The clouds over us drift together,

Blanketing us like a mother.

I see us reflected in their command,

So through the blazing fire we walked hand in hand

And as we passed through the grey we found ground.

Left there in new colours of green, yellow and brown.

5. SACRIFICE

No matter your despair,

I will be there,

In the dead of summer

And in the dead of me.

Ideally I'd bring you to somewhere warmer,

And hide all my pain so you can't see.

We'll spend so long that your worries burn away.

Purified so that anxieties never stay.

You'll hug me, keeping my pieces together

And I'll hold your hand as I melt under the pressure.

Leaving us, the whole and the martyr.

6. SCRAPED KNEES

My knees burn,

Scraped on the cement playground,

And open through the hole in my jeans.

I walk alone on my way home along the powerlines.

I can hear cars on the highway in the distance,

Adults going to and fro important meetings.

I walk with nowhere to be until sundown.

The air brushes against my wound,

Reminding me of the fun we had,

Grounders and hanging from bars,

The ground was made of lava,

And we stayed safe on burning metal.

I laugh to myself thinking about the way my friend fell,

And the scene he made burning alive.

My legs are soar from the running.

Chasing girls afraid of our kooties,

And jumping off the top of the playground thinking it would impress them.

I walk behind the houses of broken families and of new parents.

This community has never seen a month without incident,

But it is home all the same.

I stumble over the holes of prairie dogs' homes,

Potholes to remind me that I do not walk on even ground,

Nor will I ever.

People here never really make it far away,

And I guess if it's good enough for the stray animals,

It is perfect for us.

As I grow older my scars tell cautionary tales,

The powerlines lead me beyond the world I knew as a kid.

I drive to see 'important' people and do my best to imitate them.

I cry on the way home remembering the friends we had that didn't make it past the playground.

Tonight I will hold my kids close and tell them another story about the mother they will never see.

I assure them that she loved them and will always have a home with me.

They may never walk on even ground,

But they will know how to walk with scraped knees.

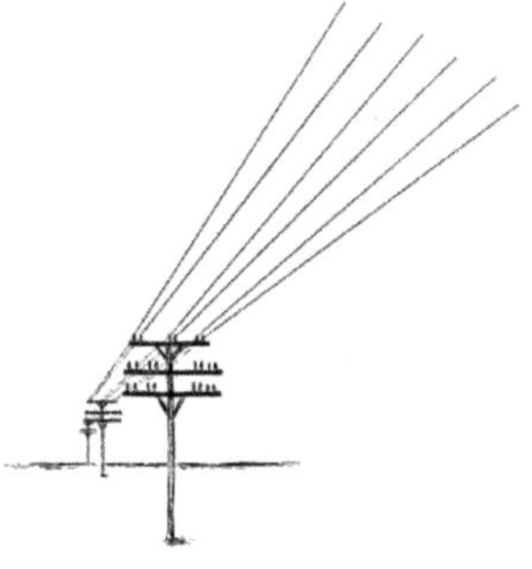

7. THE HUG BEFORE THE STORM

"It was March 12th 2020, 11:57 AM…

The last time I hugged her."

It's been several months since we've been together,

And I feel not only far from her, but far from myself.

Quarantined from intimacy and chats over coffee.

Stopping the spread of infection,

Came at the cost of my therapy.

She was my salvation,

My one true saviour from damnation,

That is: my own machination.

She gave me more than a donation,

More than just her time or sense of kindness,

She showed me myself beyond my blindness.

My vision so obscured,

I thought myself useless,

Broken down crutchless,

Abused turned to meaningless,

Injured and friendless,

Anxious,

Breathless,

Mindless,

Endless.

exasperated

"I'm here for you."

Her words ring.

Echoing through the void of hopeless.

"I miss you."

She calls to her friend she remembers happy,

As I try to remember its recipe.

I scramble to find those parts of me,

But before I do,

She appears vibrantly coloured, contrasting my dull blue.

Her form welcomes me with open arms,

And my soul is overcome with emotion.

She heals me from my own self harm,

As my tears fill not a lake, but an ocean.

She doesn't question how long I've been gone,

She only asks me to welcome a new dawn.

After so much time passed there I was,

Once again wrapped up in her embrace,

She beautifully doing what a friend does,

No matter the time or place.

Saving me, the basket case.

8. IN BED

I used to tuck my sheets so close to my body,

I'm unsure my skin could breathe.

I would hold my blankets as close to me as I could,

Thinking I could replicate the embrace of a parent.

I would roll around and make myself a small burrito boy,

So cosy and closed off no one could harm me.

The cold could not bite me and monsters couldn't pierce my fluffy armor.

I would go to sleep content that I was surrounded by warmth and love,

And I would wake the same.

Now I get into bed and have my blankets lay loosely over me,

Uncommitted to my protection,

But providing a weight to let me know I'm not alone.

My sheets are not tucked, rather I wish to breathe and air out my worries.

My bed is bigger, but it feels emptier.

My arms are no longer close to my body,

They wrap around my pillow,

Wishing I had someone in its place.

I toss and turn, unchecked by my blankets,

They become casualties of restlessness.

My dreams are caffeinated and my waking hours are filled with
sleepiness.

...

I wonder if this bed will be my final one,

Or if it will be the bed I share with the 'one',

If our kids will pounce us awake on Christmas morning.

I wonder if I will bring you breakfast in this bed,

Take care of your illnesses while you rest your head,

Spend sleepless nights and lazy mornings here with you.

There are nights where I tuck my sheets so close to my body,

That my dreams are filled by a future with you.

I can feel you close to me and hear our kids sneaking into the room.

I can hear you softly say you love me, while birds chirp outside our suburban home.

We would spend years together in love,

But I always wake,

Alone again in bed.

9. EMPATH IN LOVE

I have always felt so connected to others and their feelings.

It took many years before someone told me what I was... an empath.

Maybe that's why I feel so old,

I've experienced the emotions of 100s of lives and I've felt them 10x stronger than others.

Every worry and fear turns into my own anxiety and tears.

The feelings of hopelessness and loss is my depressiveness and stress.

I can foresee disaster with a hint of the wind,

Which echoes past trauma through a storm.

How sad I may sound to one not similar,

For it is only if you focus on the bad that this may make someone bitter.

The feelings of euphoria and elation at the sight of another loved by you is like no other.

They call me helpless in the romance department, but surely they do not know of how my heart truly dances for someone I call lover.

To have a love so overwhelming it takes over all logic and
reasoning is something to live for and something to die for.

To fall for someone new is like walking into the Garden of Eden for
the first time,

It's like finding the meaning of happiness for the second time,

It is loneliness for the last time.

Maybe it seems too glamorous to be true, too Hollywood or small
town hallmark for those out of touch, but let me tell you that
indeed there could be someone out there to make you believe too.

The first time I met her I was too in my own head to truly see her.

In our following meetings I ignored how natural it was to talk with
her.

Further interactions slowly changed the pace of our score.

Silly antics and buffoon like actions I would never do before, were
second nature when with her.

Out of my head and into her eyes, I started to feel again, what it
was that I had lost.

I couldn't tell her, but it was pretty obvious from a spectator's view,
that loving her is all I could do.

If others get puppy love, I get 'every-cute-furry-baby' love, because I fell right past that small time stuff into will you marry me, in less than a year.

When you feel more, the way I do, loving someone isn't something you do or occasionally feel,

It is something that overtakes you with emotion, passion, and is in every molecule of your being.

That whole thinking about them morning and night is 24/8.

A whole extra day is made for them just in case one gets away.

It can be minutes, days, or weeks between seeing them and it will feel like falling in love for the first time, every time they walk in the room.

They make you feel safe and look more beautiful than a sunrise at the end of a perfect day.

My spirit warms and rejuvenates in her presence,

My mind is stimulated by her conversation,

And my stomach flutters when she looks at me.

But falling in love with her has been the longest hardship I've known...

To spend everyday reminding myself we can't be together.

10. UNREQUITED LETTER

Dear You,

There will come a time when I'm gone.

I know I will have so much left unsaid,

An infinity of thoughts left unshared.

Not because I wanted to hold my tongue.

Not because I wanted to remain an enigma.

Certainly not to stay misunderstood by those who knew me.

But because I never had the chance I thought I would get...

To share with someone my intimate thoughts,

To lecture exuberantly about my theories,

To express my barely containable emotions of grandeur...

To tell her how I've always felt.

I will forever long to have been able to dance alone with you to
your favourite song.

To let our public guards down and act like sea creatures together.

To simply hold you in my arms knowing you love me almost as much as I love you.

Gosh did we come close.

Matching in every way, save for location.

We wanted the same things, but you couldn't find them in me.

Two parallel lines traveling side by side so closely, but never destined to touch.

For now and forever though,

I will always follow you.

Yours adjacently,

Me

11. 11:00 PM

The crescent moon holds gently onto the sky,

As it rises to greet those it reflects

On our backs we lie

To find spectral effects.

Living emotion is painted across the night,

Filling flowers with new breath for the day,

Our hearts create the Northern light,

Expressing feelings no words could say.

The smell of dewy grass fills our lungs,

As the cool wind brushes pine trees,

Confessional words hang on our tongues,

The silence building electricity.

Our eyes magnetized to the expanse

Infinity is sprawled around us.

As a backdrop to the stars' dance

Fireflies ascend as we discuss,

The beauty of it all.

12. MIDNIGHT MUSE

She is like the midnight rain that descends softly through the night,

With a sound so soothing your thoughts stop moving around with might.

As she speaks words that assure your safety in the arms of morning birds,

You hope you will never wash ashore, so as to stay listening to her score.

Her beauty eclipses the light of the moon passing over a clear sky.

Her grace is further highlighted by constellations she wears.

Her eyes like utopia and her heart as pure as the Sahara is dry.

She is as refreshing as spring cherries new trees bear,

Providing us with the hope of a long summer to spend together.

She is the muse that gives my words meaning

And I look forward to seeing her in the morning.

13. TIME'S WIND

Subtly the wind rustles the leaves,

Restfully you put your body to ease,

Listening to the emptiness of the night,

Urbanization is out of sight.

In this pocket of time hours can spend,

In the matter of seconds without end.

Your mind is free to roam the glade,

In this surreal space nature made.

The crickets chirp in tune to your heart,

And the owls 'hoo' behind the dark.

Embraced by the earth and grass,

Life and its worries come to pass,

Alone with yourself and comforted by silence,

Moments like these go beyond explanations of science.

Philosophy stretches to its limits to theorize,

Where art tries its best to immobilize.

There can be no replacement for such unique experience,

Only this feeling of peace provides deliverance.

Stumbling upon harmony was fortuitous,

If only humanity could be so gregarious.

Perhaps the following generations,

Will understand the serenity of land without nations.

As your life comes to pass undisciplined,

Subtly you are rustled by the wind.

14. FREE NATION

I wonder why freedom is something fought for.

Why the word was even made before.

For freedom is an innate right to be,

So why is war and bloodshed all we see.

In the pursuit of freedom there's so many casualties.

I can't help, but think of the duality

Between suffering and openness,

And how we push ourselves on closed nations,

Places where they had no need for our relations.

Can we really say they're better off with our foreign sensations?

Or have we left them without choice,

Restricting their independence with constant outside noise.

I wonder what it is to be free.

If we have the right to be without chains

Why are we subjected to change?

I suppose freedom is not to have control,

Rather we are truly fighting for life governed by principle.

Without virtue, freedom is perfect chaos,

For those living under tyranny I have pathos.

It is the age old story for the fall of oppressive leaders

And the rise of democratic dreamers,

But if you look around at the world today

Our founding philosophers would be in dismay.

Our leaders are as corrupt as they were centuries preceding

And oppression is given power by the people, against their own being.

Our own constructs become our downfall

And isn't that the perfect metaphor for us all,

As we integrate further into society

We fall deeper into our anxiety,

Living a life restricted by democracy.

15. LISTS

We fill our lives with various lists,

Whether it be a wish list, bucket list, or 'things to do',

We schedule and chain ourselves to empty boxes.

Our sense of achievement is marked on a timeline,

And we walk on a road marked by predetermined milestones.

We create new avenues to find anxiety, but neglect to pave roads to happiness.

As if by planning our lives it gives them meaning.

Life and love is not meant to be expected,

Rarely is the future awaiting for our arrival.

We have a habit of limiting ourselves to the possible in the present,

Making us unimaginative and uncomfortable with change.

We should embrace creativity and accept that the impossible is inevitable.

After all, inspiration strikes without our counsel.

16. BOTTLED

My light shines when most sleep.

Left in the night to fly with the bees,

My home is among the grass, the shrubs, and the trees.

Free to find my own path to destiny,

The sky is truly the limit,

Bounded only by my own inhibitions...

Until I wasn't.

Suddenly I couldn't move the way I could before.

Trapped seemingly by walls all around me,

I couldn't control where I moved.

After the initial panic settled down,

I started to realise it was useless to try to change the world around me.

I couldn't, even if I continued to try.

Life would move on and I would need to find my place in it.

With time I found my niche,

To light the way through darkness,

Making the unknown less hostile,

I was a firefly in a bottle.

17. ABOVE THE TUNDRA

As we lifted from the tarmac we glided across the snow soaked land.

We headed higher and higher and as we did I could see the edge of the world.

I could see how the world continued, beyond what I could imagine.

From down below it all seemed inescapable and now the sky is a broken ceiling.

We pass through the fluffy layer of cloud and a whole new world emerges.

A blank canvas for my imagination to run wild.

Towering puffs of smoke become ivory arches,

Distant cloudy consortiums look of neighbouring forestry,

And the breaks in the canvas form caverns above an abyss, back to the life I knew.

To stay up here would be to know only beauty,

But to return would be an understanding of reality.

As my mind swims through the skies in wonderment,

I drift to sleep and dream of a new life crafted by my highest of aspirations...

Only to awake once again grounded,

With a new sense of being.

18. MYSTERY OF THE GREAT

Who am I to walk amongst the greats and to spend time in their great spotlights?

Who am I to pretend as though I conquered and braved the same magnitude of fights?

For am I to stand where she stood and utter words that would pale in likeness?

To make an attempt at a similar gravitas?

Nay, it will be my humble honour to simply exist in that space for but a moment of time.

For I know a thing or two about a few things,

But I know not a lot, about a lot of things.

I am wise to my profound lack of knowledge,

Yet I am profoundly wise to another.

I suppose it is all relative.

I know I have not reached the mountain's peak,

Though I always wonder if I have reached mine.

Am I to judge the length of my journey in altitude or by distance?

What scale should I use?

Will I be thought less of if I need help?

Will I ever get to my destination if I stop to help others?

I have weighed my worth against the size of the universe and found myself insignificant.

I have travelled so far in one direction I have found myself again.

I have fallen and I have stopped, though the world kept standing and the glaciers did move.

I am here now and I brought more than myself.

Yet here I am, standing where she did and I wonder who she was.

19. FUTURE MEMORIES

Memories of a future with you embrace me like a warm welcome home.

A life I have yet to live washes over me wherever I go.

As I head closer and closer to our life together,

I see how we cook dinner together and make a mess of the kitchen.

We have candle light meals under a full moon, surrounded by string lights.

We play in the yard like high school sweethearts and tend to our fruity plants.

I see how we lay in bed talking until the sun rises and lazily slumber away on a Saturday morning.

We spend our days at work, but only truly live them when we can recount them to each other each evening.

We would sing and dance together as if every room was a ball or our last night to walk.

The dusk of a summer sun would backdrop our strolls to stargazing spots,

And in those skies I can picture a family with you.

Oh how I miss those days already.

For in the future these will be the memories I will always come back to.

20. SNOW SOAKED GRASS

Spring begins with remnants of winter.

The soil I stand on is soaked in the water of the snow that lingers...

Memories that will grow the grass green and tall.

I rake the dead leaves that suffocate the ground, hoping to reconcile the damage that has been done.

The air smells of rain and with it I am taken aback.

I remember building a blanket fort at Samantha's house and trying fries with mayo for the first time.

It's been 16 years since I've seen her, but I hope she still laughs the same way,

Soft and warm like the month of May.

As I brush past the juniper bushes I can taste the Raspberry lemonade enjoyed at summer time markets and on long road trips...

A staple for a sugar kick, which used to be fuelled by vanilla ice cream cones after soccer practice.

Oh how it was satisfying to feel the air brush our shins as we took off our pads in the car.

I pass the vent on the side of the house and smell laundry being done.

It transports me to our condo we lived in for half my life and that dingy little room where I was worried a monster waited.

Oh how I can picture every little detail of that laundry room attached to the office in the basement.

I remember the whole house at a different scale to its reality.

Of course I was little when we lived there, so everything seemed so much bigger, but I know now how poorly I understood the change in world view I would have as I grew.

As I toil in the yard I remember an entirely different life.

I had no voice when I was young or I guess I just never used it.

My family knew me to be a great listener, but terrible at conversation.

They would say, "never call Christian on the phone, you won't know if he picked up".

Though I was always there trying to learn and see what I could pick up from my family.

I always liked to imagine myself as being somewhat an amalgamation of all the people I met, whether it be the way I walk or what I do.

I did not know myself and this is what I thought identity formation was.

I did not know yet how original I could be.

Bird songs fill the air and the embrace of the wind carries me to days camping with my family.

So much was learned in the forest from bikes to s'mores,

Injuries and rules of the forest, tent building, fire tending, and much more.

In the sweat that beads down my forehead I can feel my late grandfather with me.

He always worked hard enough to warrant a few showers, whether that be from his job or tending to the yard.

His example showed me what a man should be...

Compassionate yet strong, unwavering yet understanding, but most of all, family driven.

As the sun starts to set I look up to see the same sky that draped over my family when we would take evening walks in our neighbourhood.

Walks I cherish to this day as one of the few happy memories of my parents together.

As night descends, my vision fades and the cold takes me over.

I'm flooded by the times I was alone.

When I walked to the lake with no intention of returning.

When I accepted the sting of the chemicals I ingested.

When I pressed cold steel against my skin.

Spiralling into darkness I'm caught by the big dipper.

The cosmos shines around me and Orion defends me alongside Ursa and her cub.

The moon reflects back on me the memories I had in the light of day, reminding me that while I can't feel their warmth, they are still there to see.

My life balances in the light of Libra and I fly to the safety of Andromeda on Pegasus.

Here I see my life in scale and colour.

I realize now that I am still but a seedling of grass.

With the melted memories I hold from my time under icy circumstance,

Whether the coming years be rain or shine,

I will grow green and tall.